# Sparkle and SHINE!

Trendy Earrings, Necklaces and Hair Accessories for All Occasions

by Kara L. Laughlin

raintree

a Capstone company — publishers for children

Raintree is an imprint of Capstone Global Library Limited, a company incorporated
in England and Wales having its registered office at 264 Banbury Road, Oxford, OX2
7DY – Registered company number: 6695582

**www.raintree.co.uk**
myorders@raintree.co.uk

Text © Capstone Global Library Limited 2016
The moral rights of the proprietor have been asserted.

Edited by Mari Bolte and Alesha Sullivan
Designed by Tracy Davies McCabe
Photos by Karon Dubke
Original photos © Capstone Global Library Limited 2017
Picture Research by Morgan Walters
Production by Kathy McColley
Originated by Capstone Global Library Limited
Printed and bound in China.

ISBN 978 1 4747 2387 9
20 19 18 17 16
10 9 8 7 6 5 4 3 2 1

**British Library Cataloguing in Publication Data**
A full catalogue record for this book is available from the British Library.

**Acknowledgements:**
We would like to thank the following for permission to reproduce effects:
Shutterstock: ganpanjanee, design element, Ozerina Anna,
design element, Stephanie Zieber, design element, Vaclav
Mach, design element, Yellowj, design element

Every effort has been made to contact copyright holders of material reproduced in
this book. Any omissions will be rectified in subsequent printings if notice is given to
the publisher.

# CONTENTS

# YOU'RE *one of a kind,*

## *AND YOUR ACCESSORIES SHOULD BE TOO.*

**27**

### Cross-Purpose NECKLACE

*One secret to great jewelry design: multiples! Tiles used for laying ceramic tiles. One spacer by itself may not look like much. But link them together with some colored cord, and you're crowd-sourced a beautiful necklace.*

1. Use permanent markers or nail polish to color the tile spacers as desired.
2. Wrap a piece of beading cord around a spacer to make a small X in the center. Secure by tying the ends together in the center of the X. If using spacers of different sizes, try alternating them, or stacking smaller spacers on larger spacers.
3. Cut the tails off of each knot, and then dot with a dab of glue. Make sure the tails don't show from the front.
4. Tie one piece of the toggle clasp to the 22-inch beading cord. Thread a needle onto the other end.
5. Slip the needle beneath the wrapped cord on the back of a tile spacer. Slide the tile spacer to about ½ inch (1.3 cm) away from the toggle. Tie it in place.
6. Continue stringing tile spacers onto the necklace and tying them in place. Alternate

**35**

### *Really* ROSY

*These delicate rose earrings look intricate, but they are surprisingly simple to make. Use them to add a bit of understated style to a T-shirt and jeans. Pair them with an updo and a strappy dress for a special night out.*

1. Knead a marble-sized piece of polymer clay until soft.
2. Break the clay into 16 equal balls.
3. Press one ball into a flat disk. Gently roll this disk up to make the central spiral of your rose.
4. Flatten another ball and curl it around the spiral.
5. Add six more petals to your rose. Always add in the same direction, and overlap the petals.
6. Repeat steps 3 through 5 to make a second rose.
7. Carefully cut the bottom of each rose to make it sit flat.
8. Set the roses onto a foil-lined baking sheet. Cure your roses in the oven according to package instructions.
9. When your roses have cooled completely, glue them to earring posts.

*Tip: Now that you can make clay roses, add a matching bracelet! Make 8 to 12 roses, but before you bake them, press closed jump rings into opposite sides of each rose. Connect the roses with more jump rings and add a clasp.*

**MATERIALS:**
polymer clay
tile
scissors
baking sheet
jewelry glue
earring posts

## YOU DON'T HAVE TO SPEND HUNDREDS OF POUNDS TO LOOK YOUR BEST.

With a little craft shop swag and tools from around the house, you can make stylish accessories that turn heads without emptying your purse.

You'll need a few tools if you're going to make jewellery at home. You may already have many of them. Others you may need to buy or borrow. But don't worry if you don't have a supply in your toolbox. Everything you need for these projects can be found at a craft shop, home shop or online.

1. flat-nosed pliers
2. round-nosed pliers
3. chain-nosed pliers
4. crimping pliers
5. wire cutter
6. scissors
7. sewing needle
8. beading needle
9. hammer (for hardening metal)
10. paintbrushes
11. jewellery glue
12. jump rings (open and closed)
13. clasps
14. findings
15. crimp beads
16. head pins
17. eye pins
18. jewellery hand drill

# From drink TO 'DO

*Did you know that most disposable drinking cups are made from shrinkable plastic? It's true! So the next time you're at a picnic or party, bring home your cup. No one will ever believe your latest accessory started as a drink holder!*

## MATERIALS:

baking parchment
baking tray
500 ml red plastic cup
permanent markers
hole punch

scissors
empty 500 ml
   (16-ounce) jar
bamboo skewer

*Tip: Use small, 30-millilitre (1-ounce) cups to make a barrette version of this project.*

1. Preheat oven to 120 degrees Celsius (250 degrees Fahrenheit). Lay a piece of baking parchment on a baking tray.

2. Draw a fun design on the sides of your cup with permanent markers.

3. Punch two holes on opposite sides of the cup about 1.3 centimetres (½ inch) from the rim.

4. Carefully cut away the bottom of the cup.

5. Set the cup bottom up on the baking parchment and put it in the oven.

6. The cup will collapse into a puffy disk in 3 to 5 minutes. As soon as it does, remove it from the oven. Use oven gloves to curve it around the sides of your jar.

7. Trim your bamboo skewer to 15.2 centimetres (6 inches).

8. Once the cup has cooled, slide the skewer through the holes. (You may need to re-punch the holes.)

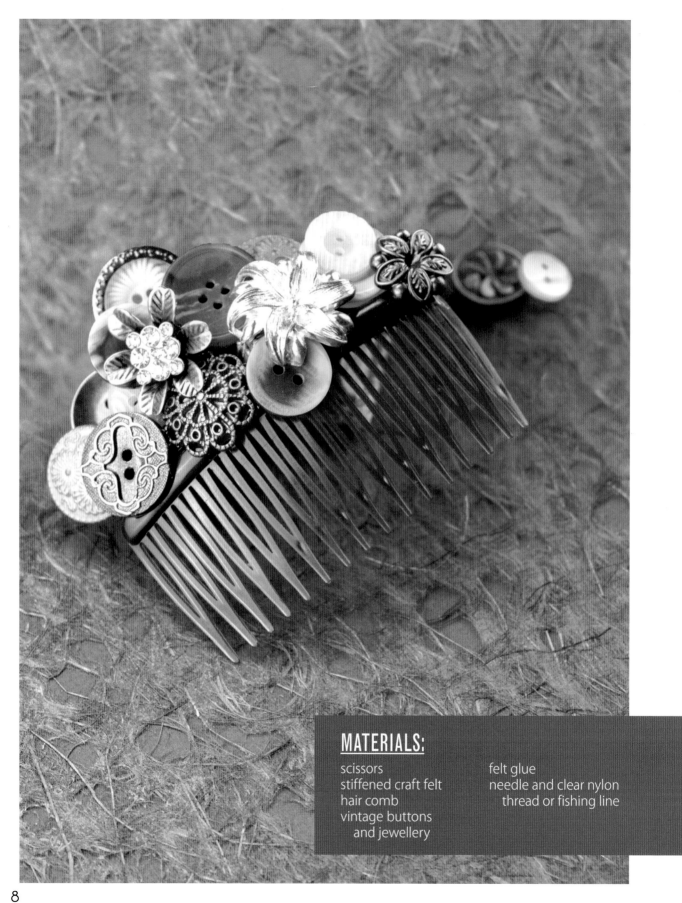

**MATERIALS:**

scissors
stiffened craft felt
hair comb
vintage buttons
  and jewellery

felt glue
needle and clear nylon
thread or fishing line

# *Vintage* GLAMOUR

*A few pieces of old costume jewellery or vintage buttons can transform hair combs from blah to bling. Search charity shops and car boot sales for your finds. Limit choices to one or two main colours to keep the project glam, not gaudy.*

*Tip: If combs don't work well in your hair, decorate a headband instead. Sew a loop of elastic to the back of the felt and slide it onto a plastic headband. You can keep it removable or glue it in place.*

1. Cut a piece of stiffened felt the same length as your hair comb.

2. Arrange buttons and jewellery pieces in a pattern on the felt. Use felt glue to glue into place. Let dry.

3. Cut away the extra felt from around the buttons and jewellery pieces.

4. Thread needle with thread or fishing line and secure the knot with felt glue.

5. Sew the felt to the comb by wrapping the thread around the top of the comb. Sew all the way across the comb and back to make sure the felt is secure. Knot the thread and cut off any excess.

6. Lay down a line of felt glue where the felt meets the top of the comb. Let the glue dry before wearing.

## MATERIALS:

serrated knife
plastic bottle with long neck
scissors
ponytail holder
sandpaper

decoupage glue
 and paintbrush
fabric
sticky-back pearls

# Rockin' HAIR CUFF

*Sometimes you want to rock a more polished ponytail.*
*Enter this hair cuff. It's great for casual hair days*
*when you want to keep a little edge.*

**1.** Use a serrated knife to cut a 5-centimetre (2-inch) tube from the bottle's neck.

**2.** Use scissors to make a cut down the length of one side of the tube.

**3.** Lightly sand the outside of the tube. Add a thin layer of decoupage glue. Press fabric into the glue to cover the tube and trim off excess. Brush more decoupage glue over the top of the fabric. Let dry completely.

**4.** Secure a ponytail holder to the inside of the tube with a piece of electrical tape. Cover the tape with more fabric and decoupage glue.

**5.** Add sticky-back pearls to the cuff.

**6.** To use your hair cuff, gather your hair into a ponytail and slip the ponytail holder over your hair. Position the cuff so that the top sits close to your scalp. Secure the ponytail holder normally.

*Tip: If you're more punk than rock, cover the tube with electric tape*
*and decorate with metal screw brads or grommets.*

# *Boho bling* HAIRBAND

*Turban-style hair wraps are super comfy and look great. This one adds to the swag factor with a sparkly chain and fabric you dye yourself.*

## MATERIALS:

tape measure
wire cutter
metal chain
beaded chain
scissors

knit cotton fabric
craft glue
no-boil fabric dye
needle and thread

*Tip: Don't use the hob method to dye the fabric. It could melt the glue.*

1. Measure the widest part of your head. Use the wire cutter to cut the metal and beaded chains to this measurement. Then cut a piece of cotton fabric, using the measurement for the length and 12.7 centimetres (5 inches) for the width.

2. Spread the fabric out on a work surface and squeeze glue in a fun pattern onto the cloth. Let the glue dry overnight.

3. Dye your cloth according to the package instructions. If some fabric puffs up while you're dying, use a wooden spoon or butter knife to push the air pocket to the edge of the fabric. That should release the bubble and let the fabric sink back into the dye. When your fabric is dyed and rinsed, but still damp, peel off the glue.

4. Wash the fabric and let it dry completely before sewing.

5. Fold your fabric along its length so that the right side of the pattern is on the inside. Sew the edges together lengthwise to make a tube. Turn the tube right-side-out.

6. Lay the chains on the fabric in an X. Sew them to the fabric where the chains cross. Sew the ends of the chains to the ends of the fabric 1.3 centimetres (½ inch) from the raw edges of the fabric.

7. Tuck 1.3 centimetres (½ inch) of one side of the tube into the other. Fold the outside fabric about 0.6 centimetres (¼ inch) under and sew the fabric together to make a circle.

# Hair sticks TO GO

*Use takeaway to take back fashion! These hair sticks will help rein in your locks when you're letting your inner wild child come out to play.*

1. Use a sharp knife to whittle a gentle point (about the shape of a dull pencil) at one end of a chopstick or stick. If using natural twigs, set them aside to dry until they are hard and strong, about three days.

2. Carve a notch into the blunt end of one stick about 0.6 centimetres (¼ inch) from the end.

3. Sand the sticks. Then rub oil over them with a clean cloth or kitchen roll.

4. Wrap wire around the notch of one stick, and then twist together to secure. Add three beads to the wire. Twist to secure the beads in a triangle at the top of the hair stick.

5. Cut the wire and weave the ends in and around the beads in a bowl shape. Wrap the ends of the wire around the notch again to secure the nest to the stick.

6. Twist a screw eye into the other stick. Attach the centre of your chain to the screw eye with a jump ring.

7. Use a jump ring to attach charms to each end of the chain.

## HOW TO WHITTLE

Whittling is a fun and safe activity as long as you take a couple of precautions.

- Check your 'circle of safety' to make sure no one is around: Hold your knife at arm's length and bring it around your body and over your head.
- Use a sharp knife. Dull knives are more likely to slip and cut you.
- Always cut away from your body.
- Don't rush! Lots of little shavings will work better than deep cuts.

# *Punchy puff* HEADBAND

*Who knew paper could be this pretty – and strong?*
*This is a great everyday headband for when you*
*want to just add a little punch to your 'do.*

3

## MATERIALS:

large saucepan
serrated knife or craft saw
12.7-cm (5-inch) wooden
    embroidery hoop
bowl or jar, about 10.2 cm
    (4 inches) wide
flower-shaped paper punch

scrapbooking paper in several
    contrasting colours
2.5-cm (1-inch) round
    paper punch
1.3-cm (½-inch) round
    paper punch
dimensional decoupage glue

1. Fill the saucepan about halfway with water. Then bring the water to a boil.

2. Cut the metal parts off the outer ring of the embroidery hoop. Boil the hoop in the water until it's flexible, about 20 minutes.

3. Use tongs to remove hoop from the water and rinse it in cold water until it's cool enough to handle. Bend the hoop and place the ends in the bowl or jar. Leave the hoop in the bowl until it's completely dry. This could take several hours, or even overnight.

4. Punch 6 flowers from each sheet of scrapbooking paper. Set the flowers on a protected work surface. Cover the flowers with dimensional decoupage glue.

5. Repeat step 4 with the round paper punches. Cover the circles with dimensional decoupage glue. Let the flowers and the circles dry completely.

6. Use decoupage glue to attach the larger circles to the flowers, and the flowers and smaller circles to the headband. Use additional glue along the underside of the flowers for added stability. Let dry completely.

17

# *Make your* MARK

*Metal stamping is easier than you think! A set of stamps, a few swings of your hammer, and you've got a personalized pendant. When you see how easy they are, you'll be making them for all of your friends.*

Tips: Practice makes perfect! Experiment with a throwaway blank before diving in.

Stamping kits and blanks can be found at craft shops. Check sales and use shop coupons to get the best deals.

1. Lightly mark the metal blank with a pencil to make sure your letters will be centred and evenly spaced. If your blanks are small, a piece or two of clear tape along the edges can help keep the blanks in place.

2. Stamp your design onto the blank. Hold the stamp straight over the blank. Hold the hammer near the head, and gently hammer the stamp once.

3. Continue stamping until the blank is decorated to your liking. Use a damp rag to rub off the pencil marks from step 1.

4. Thread the bead onto the jump ring. Then thread the metal blank onto the jump ring.

5. Hang your stamped charm off the metal choker necklace.

## MATERIALS:

2.5-cm (1-inch) circle
   paper punch
playing cards
scissors
embossing fluid
metallic embossing powder
paintbrush

hairdryer
drawing pin
clear nail polish
jewellery pliers
jump rings
30.5-cm (12-inch) piece
   of necklace chain

# Dealing up DESIGN

*The next time you discover a few cards missing from your favourite deck, don't toss the rest. Show off the detailed designs by incorporating them into this scalloped necklace.*

1. Punch 8 circles from playing cards. Then cut them in half.

2. Pour embossing fluid onto a paper plate. Dip the cut edges of the half circles into the fluid. Then dip the edges with embossing powder. Use a dry paintbrush to dust off any excess powder. Heat the powder with a hairdryer until the powder melts and turns shiny.

3. Use a drawing pin to poke a hole in each of the top corners of the card pieces. Add a drop of clear nail polish to each hole. Let dry.

4. Use jewellery pliers to thread a jump ring through one of the holes. Use the jump rings to join 10 card pieces.

5. Repeat to make a second chain of six card pieces. Attach the ends of the chains to one another.

6. Attach the necklace chain to the jump rings at the ends of the card pieces.

*Tip: Open and close those jump rings correctly! Use two pairs of pliers and twist the ends perpendicular to the ring. When you twist back to close, wobbling the ends will help keep it closed.*

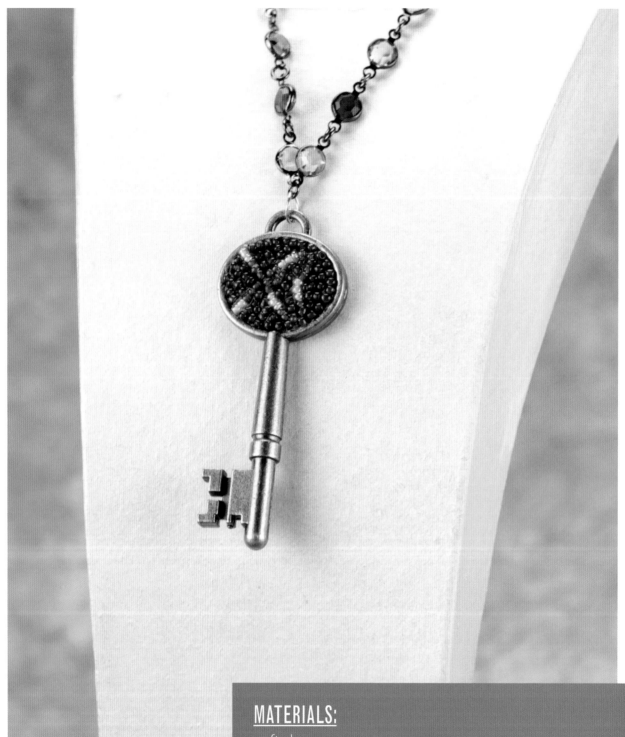

## MATERIALS:

craft glue
pendant with bezel setting
foil-lined seed beads, size 12
tweezers
loose seed beads

sponge
powdered tile grout or
  mosaic grout
decorative chain or string
  of seed beads with a clasp

# Magical MOSAIC

*Don't you just love it when all the little things come together? Foil-lined beads make this pendant sparkle, and mosaic grout keeps them in place.*

Tip: If you don't have grout handy, you can use clear resin. Make sure you pop any air bubbles before you let the resin dry.

1. Use glue to draw a shape on the inside of the bezel setting.

2. Lay your beads on the glue. Use tweezers to nudge the string into a smooth shape. Let the glue dry.

3. Remove the excess beads from your design. Fill the rest of the bezel setting with glue, and add loose beads in a second colour to cover the rest of the bezel setting. Let dry.

4. Follow package instructions to mix grout. Apply grout evenly to the beads. It's okay if the beads don't show through or look dusty.

5. Allow the grout to dry for one hour. Wipe off excess grout with a damp sponge.

6. Let grout set for another day, then wipe again with a damp sponge.

7. Hang the pendant on a chain or string of beads.

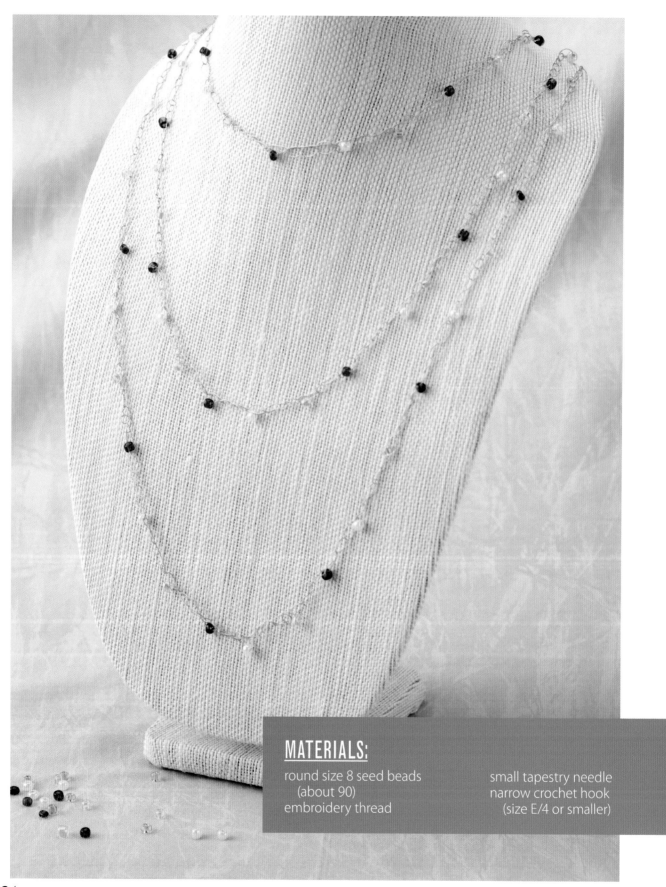

## MATERIALS:

round size 8 seed beads
(about 90)
embroidery thread

small tapestry needle
narrow crochet hook
(size E/4 or smaller)

24

# Beauty and the BEADS

*Wear this fibre necklace long, or wrap it around your neck a few times for a layered look. It's amazing how pretty slipping one loop over another can be – when you do it several hundred times!*

1. Thread beads onto your spool of embroidery thread with your beading needle.

2. Tie a loop in the end of the thread, and put the loop on your crochet hook.

3. Twist thread around your crochet hook and slip the first loop off the hook. This is a single crochet.

4. After five single crochets, push a bead up so that it gets wrapped around the hook. When you slip the loop off the hook, slip the loop over the bead as well.

5. Continue making single crochets, and adding a bead every fifth stitch, until the necklace measures 122 centimetres (48 inches).

6. Slip the hook back into the beginning of your chain. Wrap the hook as usual, and then slip both loops off the hook. Cut the thread away from the spool and pull the end through.

7. With your tapestry needle, weave the end of the thread back into the necklace.

*Tip: Get a very different look with different materials. Try using satin or organza ribbon with 0.6-centimetre (¼-inch) painted glass beads for a more romantic look. You can even crochet a chain from beading wire.*

## MATERIALS:

permanent markers or nail polish
   in various colours
X-shaped tile spacers
beading cord
clear glue

toggle clasp
56-cm- (22-inch-) long piece
   of beading cord
tapestry needle
beads of various sizes

# Cross-purpose NECKLACE

*One secret to great jewellery design: multiples! Tile spacers are used for laying ceramic tiles. One spacer by itself may not look like much. But link them together with some coloured cord, and you've crowd-sourced a beautiful necklace.*

1. Use permanent markers or nail polish to colour the tile spacers as desired.

2. Wrap a piece of beading cord around a spacer to make a small X in the centre. Secure by tying the ends together in the centre of the X. If using spacers of different sizes, try alternating them, or stacking smaller spacers on larger spacers.

3. Cut the tails off of each knot, and then dot with a dab of glue. Make sure the tails don't show from the front.

4. Tie one piece of the toggle clasp to the 56-centimetre beading cord. Thread a needle onto the other end.

5. Slip the needle beneath the wrapped cord on the back of a tile spacer. Slide the tile spacer to about 1.3 centimetres (½ inch) away from the toggle. Tie it in place.

6. Continue stringing tile spacers onto the necklace and tying them in place. Alternate with beads, if desired.

7. Tie the end of the cord to the second part of the toggle clasp. Cut off ends and glue the clasp knots.

*Tip: Tying knots gets tricky when you've got a few crosses strung. To make it easier, let your needle do the work. After you've strung the tile spacer, slide your needle through the wrapped cord to make a loop. Slip the needle through the loop, and then pull tight to knot your tile spacer in place.*

## MATERIALS:

small lock charm
122-cm (48-inch) chain with
    round links at least 0.1 cm
    (⅜ inch) in diameter

0.6-cm- (¼-inch-) wide
    leather cord
coordinating key charm
two 0.6 cm beads

# Lariat lock DOWN

*This lariat necklace is key to having a little versatility in your jewellery collection. Since it adjusts to any neckline, you'll always have a lock on a great look.*

1. Slip the lock charm onto the chain and fold the chain so that the ends are together with the lock hanging at the other end.

2. Cut a 2.4-metre (8-foot) piece of cord. Starting at the lock end, thread the cord through links on either side of the chain. Even out the cord so that both ends are the same length.

3. Thread the left cord down through the next open link on the right chain. Then thread the right cord down the next open link on the left chain.

4. Your cord should be on the underside of the chain. Cross the cords and send them back up through the next links.

5. Continue lacing the cord through the chain all the way down. Tie a knot, but do not cut the ends.

6. Slip the working end of the chain through the lock's handle. Then tie the key to the working end of the chain.

7. Tie a bead to the end of each cord, then cut off the end.

## MATERIALS:

polymer clay
drinking straws cut into
    7.6-cm (3-inch) pieces
foil
baking tray
scissors
51-cm- (20-inch-) long chain

51-cm- (20-inch-) long piece of
    1.3-cm- (½-inch-) wide ribbon
4 ribbon crimps
14-mm jump rings
necklace clasp
pendant

# In a TWIST

*Here's a new twist on a romantic ribbon necklace.*
*The handmade spiral beads add a splash of colour*
*and fun – perfect for a night out with friends.*

1. Pull off a marble-sized piece of polymer clay, and knead it until it's soft.

2. Roll the clay into a snake about 0.6 centimetres (¼ inch) in diameter. Wrap the snake in a tight spiral around a drinking straw, and set onto a foil-lined baking tray.

3. Repeat steps 1 and 2 to make three more beads.

4. Bake the clay beads according to the package instructions.

5. When the beads have baked and cooled, slide them off the straws.

6. Gather the two ribbons and chain together. Insert them into the top of a spiral bead. Twist the spiral around the ribbon and chain until they are completely inside the spiral. Add the rest of your beads the same way.

7. Add a ribbon crimp to each of your ribbon ends.

8. Attach the ribbon crimps and chain to your clasp with a jump ring. Use another jump ring to attach the pendant.

*Tip: These beads work well alone too! Before you bake them, make loops in the ends for jump rings. You can cluster five or seven together for a squiggly pendant, or link them together lengthwise for a fun bracelet.*

**MATERIALS:**

jewellery pliers
15-gauge dead soft copper wire
round-nosed pliers

¼-inch (0.6-cm) beads
head pins
pencil

# *Edgy* EAR CUFF

*Ear cuffs give you the look of a piercing without being permanent. Next time you want to add a little edge to your look, slip this on and rock out.*

1. Using jewellery pliers, bend the copper wire in half.

2. About 3.8 centimetres (1½ inches) from the first bend, bend the wire back in the other direction. Repeat on the other side.

3. Make two more bends, about 2.5 centimetres (1 inch) further down the wire on each side. The wire should look like a tight zigzag with long ends.

4. About 2.5 centimetres (1 inch) beyond the last bends, bend the end of the wire at a 90-degree angle. On the left side, shape the wire into a spiral.

5. Make two soft bends in the left side of the wire. Use round-nosed pliers to make a loop at the end.

6. Thread your bead on a head pin. Curl the head pin closed around the wire loop.

7. Bend the five prongs of the zigzag up and around a pencil.

8. Fit your ear cuff around the top of your ear, making sure the spiral and the drop bead are visible from the front.

*Tip: Everyone's body is different, and that goes for ears too! If your cuff is too loose or too tight, you may need to start again and adjust the length of wire between the hairpin bends. Or you may want to try a thinner wire (20-gauge).*

polymer clay        baking tray
penknife            jewellery glue
foil                earring posts

# *Really* ROSY

*These delicate rose earrings look intricate, but they are surprisingly simple to make. Use them to add a bit of understated style to a T-shirt and jeans. Pair them with an updo and a strappy dress for a special night out.*

**3**  **4**  **7**

1. Knead a marble-sized piece of polymer clay until soft.

2. Break the clay into 16 equal balls.

3. Press one ball into a flat disc. Gently roll this disc up to make the central spiral of your rose.

4. Flatten another ball and curl it around the spiral.

5. Add six more petals to your rose. Always add in the same direction, and overlap the petals.

6. Repeat steps 3–5 to make a second rose.

7. Carefully cut the bottom of each rose to make it sit flat.

8. Set the roses onto a foil-lined baking tray. Cure your roses in the oven according to package instructions.

9. When your roses have cooled completely, glue them to earring posts.

*Tip: Now that you can make clay roses, add a matching bracelet! Make 8 to 12 roses, but before you bake them, press closed jump rings into opposite sides of each rose. Connect the roses with more jump rings and add a clasp.*

## MATERIALS:

16 to 20 thin gauge (8- to 12-mm) jump rings

two 2.5-cm- (1-inch-) long pieces of brass chain, 0.3 cm (⅛ inch) in diameter

two 3.8-cm- (1½-inch-) long pieces of brass chain, 0.3 cm (⅛ inch) in diameter

two 6.4-cm- (2½-inch-) long pieces of silver chain, 0.6-cm (¼ inch) in diameter

four 3.2-cm- (1¼-inch-) long pieces of silver chain, 0.3 cm (⅛ inch) in diameter

two 3.2-cm- (1¼-inch-) long pieces of copper chain, 0.6 cm (¼ inch) in diameter

two 5-cm- (2-inch-) long pieces of copper chain, 0.6 cm (¼ inch) in diameter

two 5-cm-long pieces of copper chain, 0.3 cm (⅛ inch) in diameter

two 3.8-cm-long pieces of copper chain, 0.3 cm (⅛ inch) in diameter

two pairs jewellery pliers

6 top-drilled crystal teardrop beads

ear wires

# Crystal CHANDELIERS

*When your outfit calls for high drama, break out these chandelier earrings. The mixed metals mean you can wear them with most fashion styles. Bonus: they're a great way to upcycle old necklaces.*

1. Use a jump ring to attach a 2.5-centimetre- (1-inch-) long piece of brass chain to a 3.2-centimetre (1¼-inch) piece of silver chain.

2. Repeat to attach a 3.2-centimetre- (1¼-inch-) long piece of silver chain with a matching piece of copper chain. Make pairs of 3.8-centimetre (1½-inch) chains and 5-centimetre (2-inch) chains in the same way.

3. Arrange your chain pairs so that the shorter pieces are on the outside and the longer ones are in the centre. You will have one 6.4-centimetre (2½-inch) piece of silver chain in the centre.

4. Use the jump ring to attach the chains to the earring through the holes on the bottom.

5. Thread a jump ring through one of the crystal beads. Attach the bead to the bottom of the longest chain. Attach two more crystal beads to the next longest chains.

6. Hang your earring on the loop at the bottom of the ear wire. Use pliers to close up the loop.

7. Repeat steps 1–7 to make a second earring.

*Tip: For a retro look, skip the crystals and paint the chains with brightly coloured nail polish or enamel paint.*

# Ten-minute HOOPS

*Hoops are the blue jeans of jewellery – you can wear them every day, and they go with anything. Make a few pairs with different beads, and you'll always have something to wear with your favourite outfits.*

4

1. Wrap a piece of wire completely around the spool one time. Add 1.3 centimetres (½ inch), then cut.

2. With round-nosed pliers, turn the extra 1.3 centimetres (½ inch) of wire into a loop.

3. Grasp the loop with flat-nosed pliers and bend it away from the hoop at a 45-degree angle. Set aside.

4. Thread a head pin through one of the large beads. Use round-nosed pliers to make a loop at the top of the head pin.

5. String four seed beads onto the hoop. Add the large bead. Then string four more seed beads.

6. Use the flat-nosed pliers to bend up the free end of the hoop. Trim off any extra wire and smooth the cut end with a nail file.

7. Gently hammer each side of the hoop flat.

8. Repeat steps 1–7 for the second earring.

## TEMPER, TEMPER!

Wire has to be bendy enough to work with, but not so bendy that it loses its shape. Fortunately, there's a way to have your wire flexible when you're working it, and firm when you finish. It's called tempering.

Here are a few ways to temper your jewellery wire:

• pull the wire straight with nylon-nosed pliers

• bend it as you work with it

• hammer it

Be careful! If you work the metal too much, it becomes brittle and can break.

## MATERIALS:

wool roving in two colours
hot water
dish soap
needle that will fit through the
    holes in your beads

thread
seed beads
closed jump rings
ear wires

# Felting FUN

*When you think of wool, you probably think jumpers or socks. But wool is great for jewellery too. It's strong, inexpensive and easy to decorate. These earrings start off as little more than fluff. With a little work, though, you'll have bits of felt perfect for fashion.*

1. Pull four to five pieces of wool roving into a strip about 7.6-by-1.3-centimetres (3-by-½-inches). Tie the wool into a loose knot.

2. Dip the wool in hot, soapy water. Roll the knot around in your hands for about 15 minutes, until it's tight and round.

3. Pull about twice as much roving as before and dip it in the water. Make a long teardrop shape by gently rolling the wool back and forth.

4. Repeat steps 1–3 for the second earring. Allow felted pieces to dry for two days.

5. Sew seed beads onto the felt pieces.

6. Attach closed jump rings to the top and bottom of each felt ball.

7. Sew each teardrop to the bottom jump rings. Attach earring wires to the top jump rings.

*Tip: If your wool shapes keep breaking open, start over with a new piece of roving and be gentler when you roll it. Too much pressure will felt the piece before it has time to knit together into the shape that you want.*

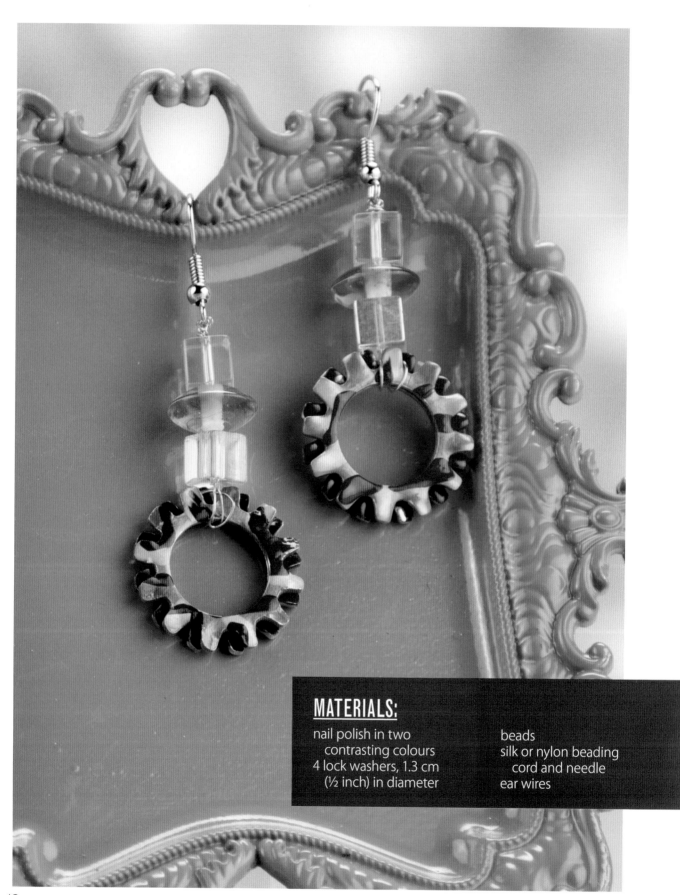

## MATERIALS:

nail polish in two
  contrasting colours
4 lock washers, 1.3 cm
  (½ inch) in diameter

beads
silk or nylon beading
  cord and needle
ear wires

# *Sunburst* DANGLES

*Jewellery supplies don't just come from the craft shop. These earrings are made of lock washers, found at hardware and home improvement shops. Make these baubles bright with a pop of colour and a few pretty beads.*

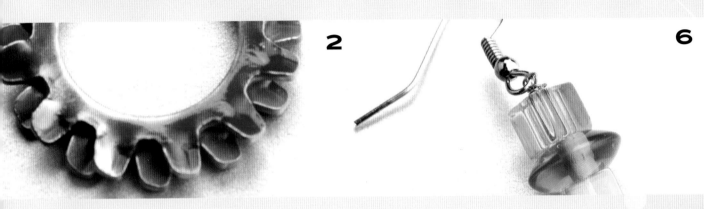

1. Use nail polish to paint one pair of washers. Paint the second pair of washers with the second colour. Let dry.

2. Position one lock washer over another of the other colour. Their prongs should alternate to make a two-colour starburst shape.

3. Fold a 45.7-centimetre (18-inch) piece of beading cord in half. Slip the centre through one pair of lock washers, and then pass the ends through to make a slipknot.

4. Tie one end of the cord to the needle. Thread three beads onto the cord, then pass the needle through an ear wire. Send the needle back down through the beads and tie it to the other end of the beading cord.

5. Send the needle back up through the beads, and cut the cord between two beads so that the end disappears between them.

6. Thread the other end of the beading cord and hide its end between the beads in the same way.

7. Repeat for the second earring, alternating which colour washer is on top, if desired.

## SOURCING OUTSIDE THE BOX

Hardware shops aren't the only places hiding jewellery equipment in plain sight! Next time you're in one of these shops, keep a lookout for these great components:

hardware shop: washers, nuts, zip ties, fan pulls, tile spacers, tile grout, bungee cords, keys, chains

office supply shop: metal brads, paper clips, metal and paper price tags, pencils, safety pins

fabric shop: zips, buttons, buckles, plastic cord guide rings, ribbons, fringe, tassels

electronics shop: resistors, LED lights, copper wire, electrical tape, PVC tape

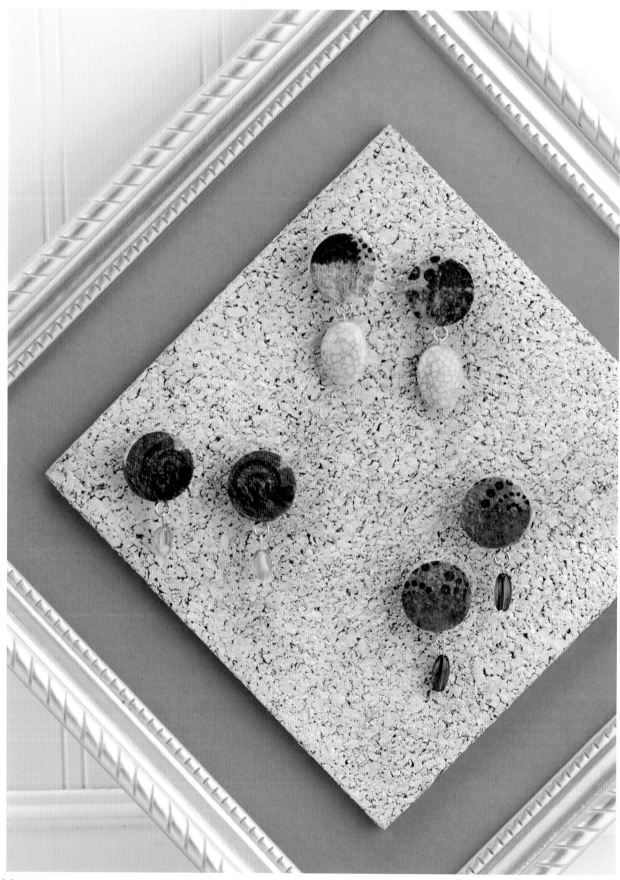

# Quirky cork POSTS

*Slices of cork are the perfect canvases for rubber stamps and ink. These earrings are so adaptable, you could make several pairs with completely different looks.*

**4**

## MATERIALS:

cork bottle stopper
serrated knife
alcohol ink
patterned rubber stamp
   and stamp pad
permanent markers
tissue paper
decoupage glue

two 0.6-cm (¼-inch)
   screw eyes or head pins
jewellery glue
2 round or oval beads
2 eye pins
round-nosed pliers
earring posts and backs

1. Cut two 0.3-centimetre- (⅛-inch-) thick pieces of cork with a serrated knife.

2. Add a drop of alcohol ink to two or three places on the cork discs. Let dry.

3. Ink your rubber stamp and press it onto the cork so that the top half of the cork is covered in the pattern. Use permanent markers to colour in the pattern on the cork, if desired.

4. Tear two pieces of tissue paper into 2.5-centimetre (1-inch) squares. Lay the tissue paper across the bottom halves of the corks. Paint the paper with decoupage glue and wrap the edges around the cork. Let dry.

5. Gently twist screw eyes into the bottom edges of the cork discs. Secure with a dot of jewellery glue.

6. Thread beads onto the eye pins. Use round-nosed pliers to loop them through the screw eye.

7. Secure earring posts to the backs of the cork circles with jewellery glue.

**MATERIALS:**

alcohol inks in two colours
2 metal blanks with a hole
  at the top
cotton swabs
jump rings
ear wires

chandelier findings with
  three links
14 0.3-cm (⅛-inch) beads
14 head pins
round-nosed pliers

# *Rainy day* DANGLES

*Need a lift on a grey day? Try on some fab earrings!
The back discs of these earrings may look like puddles in
the rain, but with these pretty dangles in your ears, you'll
be walking on sunshine all day long.*

**2**

**6**

1. Place one drop of alcohol ink onto each blank. Add one or two drops of the other colour. Use a cotton swab to push the ink around on the metal. When you have the look you want, let it dry.

2. Attach a jump ring to the top of a blank.

3. Thread an earring wire and a chandelier finding onto the jump ring. Thread another jump ring onto the chandelier finding.

4. Place a bead on a head pin, then use the pliers to close the head pin. Repeat to make six more beads.

5. Hang one bead off the jump ring from step 2. Add three more beads to the second jump ring.

6. Use more jump rings to hang a bead onto each of the chandelier finding's links.

# Find out more

*Accessories for All* (Be Creative), Anna Claybourne
(Franklin Watts, 2015)

*Jewellery* (Craft Smart), Laura Torres (QED, 2013)

*Jewellery Fantasy: A Guide for Creative Girls*, Marcelina
Grabowska-Friday (Nanook Books, 2015)

# About the author

Kara Laughlin is the author of more than two dozen books for young people. When
she isn't writing, she spends her time making embroidered jewellery and teaching
children about writing, making things and the natural world. She lives in Virginia,
USA, with her husband, three children, one dog and two guinea pigs.

# Books in this series: